Fun Days
on South Padre Island

Alligator

by

Pat McGrath-Avery & Joyce Faulkner

Copyright: 2013
Text & Photos by Pat McGrath-Avery
Design by Joyce Faulkner

All Rights Reserved. No part of this book may be reproduced or transmitted in any form or by any means, electronic or mechanical, including photocopying, recording, or by an information storage and retrieval system (except by a reviewer who may quote brief passages in a review to be printed in a magazine, newspaper or on the Internet) without permission in writing from the publisher.

ISBN: 978-1-937958-48-0 (softcover)
LCCN: 2013908807

Red Engine Press
Bridgeville, PA
Printed in the United States

Thank you to Bonnie Lazarus, Dolphinwhisper Scarlet Colley, Lucinda (Sandy Feet) Wierenga, and Steve Hathcock for sharing their photos.

Note to parents: The destinations and services in this book are only a sampling of Port Isabel and South Padre Island's activities. Kids can take surfing, kiting, fishing, eco-tours, and sand castle-building lessons. Several businesses offer a variety of water sports activities.

Alligator

You will love the boardwalk at South Padre Island Birding Center. You can climb to the top of the center and look out over the island and Port Isabel. Look for the lighthouse! On the second floor, there is a museum about the critters that live on the island and in the Gulf.

How many critters did YOU see?

Places
Whale Wall and Nature Walk at the Convention Center
7355 Padre Blvd

The Convention Center is next door to the Birding Center. The Whale Wall mural covers three walls. This painting by Robert Wyland is called "Orcas off the Gulf of Mexico."

Rescued Turtle

Ila, the Turtle Lady

Last one in the water is a rotten egg!

Hatchling Release

Things to Do on South Padre Island
Build Sand Castles

"Did YOU build a sand castle today?"

Learn to Build a Sand Sculpture

A Sand Frog!

Things to Do on South Padre Island
Enjoy our Beaches

Parasailing

Pelican

But Keep them Clean

Pick up your trash. We need your help to keep our beaches beautiful.

Things to Do on South Padre Island
Things to Ride

Go-Karts at Gravity Park

Go for a Ride on the Beach!

Go on an Eco-Tour!

Want to Race?

Rozzi and dolphins!

Rozzi and an old friend!

Things to Do on South Padre Island
Local Plants and Wild Life

How many of these plants and animals did YOU see on the island?

Hummingbird

Hibiscus

Yucca

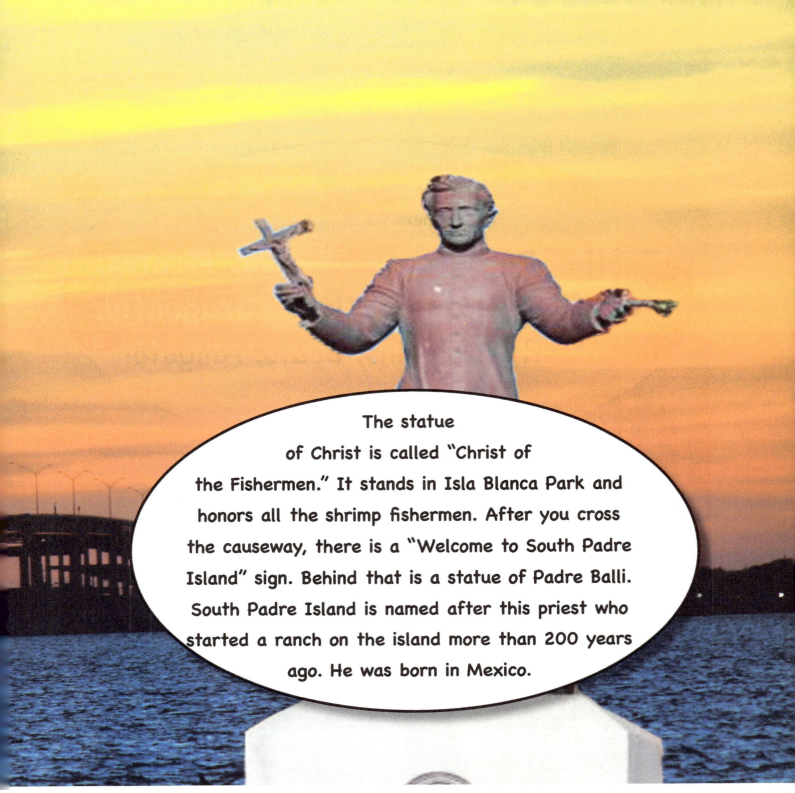

The statue of Christ is called "Christ of the Fishermen." It stands in Isla Blanca Park and honors all the shrimp fishermen. After you cross the causeway, there is a "Welcome to South Padre Island" sign. Behind that is a statue of Padre Balli. South Padre Island is named after this priest who started a ranch on the island more than 200 years ago. He was born in Mexico.

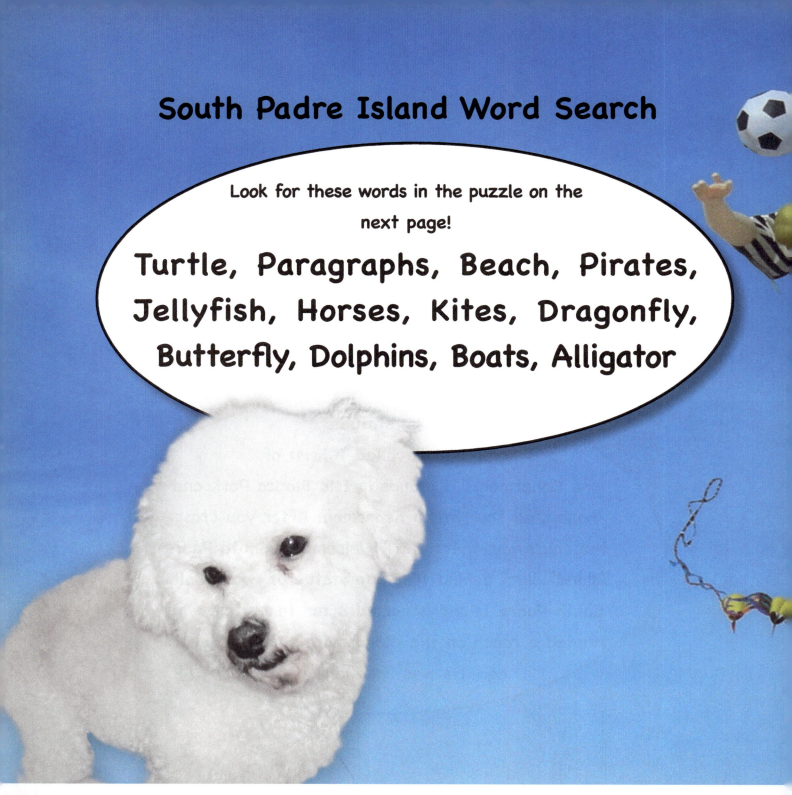

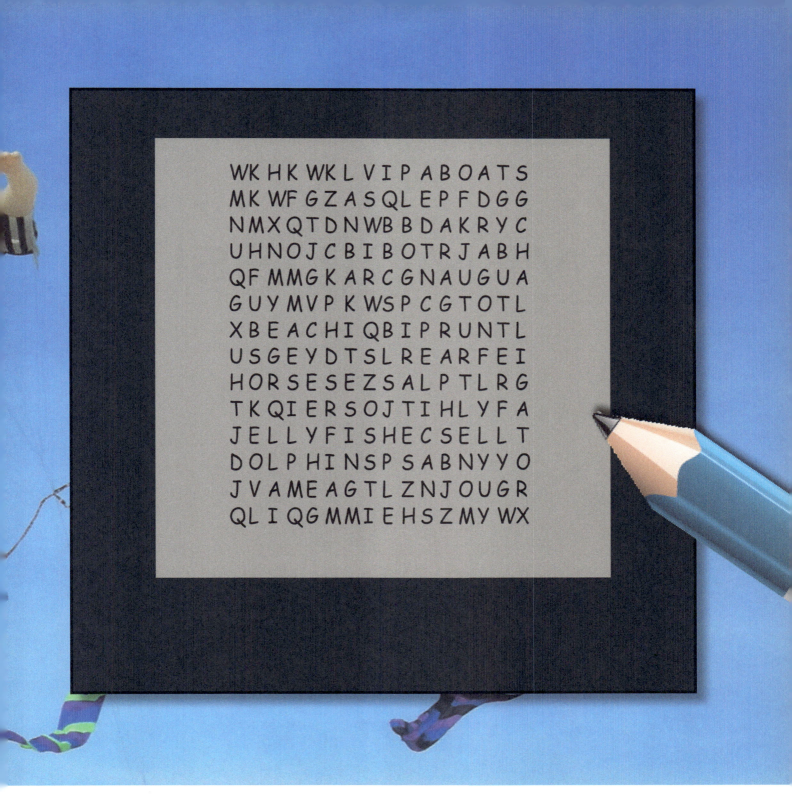

CPSIA information can be obtained at www.ICGtesting.com
Printed in the USA
LVOW01s0731220813

348927LV00004B/11/P

9 781937 958480